Destination Mutable

John H. Baillie

Library of Congress Control Number 2008927127

ISBN 978-0-9717468-7-9

First Edition

www.greenfrigatebooks.com

. Distributed by Independent Publishers Group

Baillie, John H.
Destination Mutable

1.Poetry. 2. Health. 3. Nature.

Cover Photo: Garden Path Uncertainty, R. L. France

Book Design: Opaque Design and Print Production

Printing this book on recycled stock has saved:
4.224 trees, 1813.5 gallons of water, 729.472 kw hrs electricity
199.808 lbs solid waste, 392.832 greenhouse gasses

Printed in Canada

Contents

Note From the Publisher

Foreword

I

1.   *The time was rich*

2.   Being and Nothingness Koan

3.   Finding Memory

4.   landscape

5.   Unnatural Selection

6.   while distracted …

7.   Who's Driving the Hearse?

8.   Bricks and Mirrors

9.   entropy

10.   If …

11.   Not a Morning Person

12.   hibiscus

13.   herbs afoot

14.   mutter, mutter

18.   Iron in the Broccoli

19.   Employment Opportunity

20.   The Long Sky

21.   sunrise

22.   Catch the Drift

23.   A Middle Earth Memory

24.   The Spinning Tree

25.   The Thunder of Leaves

II.

26.   *soon after*

27.   My Disappointment With the Moon

28.   Fire Lake

29.   In the Late Afternoon

30.   The Ghost Across the Hall

31.   Ophelia Rises

32.   Into the Pool Of –

34.   Thea's Canyon

35.   and then …

36.   choices

37.   scintilla

38.   Physics

39.   Godiva Night

41.   Cooling Down, Just

42.   the signal

43.   If you're grinning …

44.   to breathe in a hostile climate

45.   Twice the Speed of Roses

46.   familiar song

48.   Heartscape with Water

III.

49.   *how long did I wait here*

50.   The catherine wheel

51.   Kids in Circles

52.   Giving Up Control

53.   In the Face of the Morning News

54.   one puzzle, many pieces, no clues

55.   Owl

59.   The Buddha Pool

60.   The Specialist

62.   Charlie Parker

63.   the jazzman in the Dutch window

64.   Running Through Glass

66.   On The Borderline

67.   The Visit

68.   What I Fear

69.   Sunrose

70.   traveling wrongward

71.   The Thirteenth

73.   Detachable Unit

74.   *Syrian goddess suite*

        In the garden

        Ereshkigal, my companion

        I've seen the angry dead

81.   Crow

82.   life without oceans

IV.

83. *heading south*

84. Spring Dream

86. Three Variations on an Icon: Blackbeard's Flag

89. Life's Like That

90. Points of Viewing

91. Indistinctly Extinct

92. Magic Show

94. Climbing Mount Everest With a Blonde Supermodel Spanish Mathematician

97. Tympanic Zen Brain

99. There Must Be A Punchline

100. Anubis on the Prairies

101. deus ex vampira

102. Hot Fish Music

103. Standing Mast-Head

104. The Cinnamon Whale

106. The Ancient Sands of Egypt

107. teaching her how to fly

108. Dr. Hoffman's Happy Gene Machine

110. Compulsion

113. Destination Mutable

115. Waking Up Gautama

About Green Frigate Books

Other Green Frigate Books

To Sam and Nurit,
for having the best stories and songs.

Note From the Publisher

The muse whose wise words inspired the creation of Green Frigate Books was an artist, a master wordsmith, a poet who passionately believed that "there is no frigate like a book / to take us lands away". Indeed. Emily Dickinson lived her entire life within one hundred miles of her birthplace in Amherst, Massachusetts, but she traveled the world through books. And the journeys changed her. And we are the beneficiaries.

If you love books, you love the sound and shape of words. Words on the page have an indelible power, a power to transport us, and transform us. Such journeys can be far reaching, traversing the exotic landscapes of the external world, or they can be interior journeys – journeys of the mind that are no less exotic, and often daunting precisely because they strike so close to home, so close to the bone of life.

Green Frigate Books has championed, and will continue to champion, artists who wish to conceptually sail and explore the far horizons of the natural and built environments, and the relations of humans within them. We are also passionately committed to bringing new artists – undiscovered voices – to an audience. The poetic voice is especially important in this regard. We have ventured into this territory before, albeit tentatively. Occasional poems occur in *Profitably Soaked: Thoreau's Engagement with Water* (R. L. France, 2003), *A Wanderer All My Days: John Muir in New England* (J. P. Huber, 2007), *Ultreia! Onward! Progress of the Pilgrim* (R. L. France, 2007), and *Uncommon Cents: Thoreau and the Nature of Business* (R. M. Abbott, 2008). And poetry is used as an important element to amplify the arguments in *Deep Immersion: The Experience of Water* (R. L. France, 2004) and *Conscious Endeavors: Business, Society and the Journey to Sustainability* (R. M. Abbott, 2009). Finally, the prophetic wisdom of four-thousand year old Mesopotamian poetry is at the core of *Wetlands of Mass Destruction: Ancient Presage for Contemporary Ecocide in Southern Iraq* (R. L. France, 2007).

Still, a complete book of poetry by a modern writer has eluded us. Until now…

Foreword

John H. Baillie is a poet with a rare voice, and in *Destination Mutable* he reminds us of the singular beauty of poetry as a means of communication. He also deftly reminds us that the most interesting landscapes lie within ourselves.

Nature, love, death, and the imagination. This is the landscape, both physical and metaphysical, of the artist. If the writer's goal is to interpret the world, one eye looking back, the other forward, the most intimate manifestation of this goal is to draw meaning from a life on the edge of death; to read the map of our life, as Borges would have us, written in the creases of our face, or indeed, the folds of our heart. It is this intimate landscape that John Baillie bravely chronicles in *Destination Mutable*. In the face of acute pain brought on by a rare heart disorder, Baillie explored his relationship with nature, love, death, and the imagination through poetry. Over a five-year period, much of it in the shadow world between life and death, he tapped his creative impulses to make sense of his rapidly changing world, his diminished physical self, and the nature of *being*. In this dark wood of the mind and body, when he was neither truly alive nor dead, neither here not there, Baillie discovered that the journey of life endlessly changes through the very act of living, and the choices we make along the way. Through poetry he struck a blow against his, and our, indifference, our ignorance, our inability to consistently pay attention to the world around us – maladies that too often consign us to stagnation and misunderstanding.

Seamus Heaney has said that poetry has both practical and poetic dimensions – the former teach us how to live, the latter how to live more abundantly. I think of this as I hold John Baillie's poems in my mind, turning their meaning and inspiration over like smooth stones. His relationships with people, nature, and most especially, his sense of what it means to be alert and alive in the world – rendered so nakedly on the page – are a potent reminder of the power of poetry to communicate essential truths about life

– and how to live. They evoke, as all poems must, emotion, inspiration and even awe. In *Destination Mutable* he has given us a rare glimpse of what Emily Dickinson meant when she described the miracle of words that is a prancing page of poetry.

—Robert M. Abbott, in the shadow of the Rocky Mountains,
2009

The time was rich, we mined it like gypsies,
weaving crimson, indigo, perfect white into firelight.
Everyone who spoke spoke rightly, every word was heard.
We told each other the absolute point of things, but not to worry,
there was no point, so then there was, and we were all warmed
by this knowledge. Then each in turn wrapped all others in beauty,
beauty all eyes for once were open to see. Relations were good.
We did not love, but we smiled. And then the windows opened,
we flew away like birds, the moment over but the memory fixed,
and each of us would write of what we knew ...

Being and Nothingness Koan

I will take you to that mountain,
but that mountain is not there,
that mountain that is my mountain.
There the sunshine will be bright upon us,
but the sun does not shine;
we bask so warm and content in its light.
There we will know perfect peace,
but living in such misery
we must kiss, you and I,
when I am so alone.
Our hearts will be so full
we will feel utterly lost and empty
and finally find contentment

your touch — a moment — a flower — the rain — my eyes

first there is a mountain,
then there is no mountain,
then there ...

Finding Memory

Numbers fall in frantic repetition
as time escapes my grasp
ever more completely.
I panic in the face of arbitrary deadlines
striving to see the pebble,
for in the stone lies memory.
I will start small
before daring to perceive the mountain —

but the pebble lies beneath glass.
I stare intently but perceive only blackness

reflecting me back at me,
without life, without movement,
finally, without memory ... I forget.
Then perceive a wet motion, glistening,
a gleam of light ...
I begin to see. Not glass. Water.
Rippling with gentle life.
No distractions now,
only focus,
on the water's soft song.
Blurred by movement, I begin to perceive
the beauty of the pebble.

Forget the necessity of time
and arbitrary endings.
In the song of water streaming
over stone memory is forever alive.

Calming strength begins to flow ...

landscape

I shape the land that is me,
mixing equally of water, sand, and stone.
Then come trees, and grass, and moss
and the rich rare earth that lies beneath,
the rich rare earth that is black and fertile
and in which I must cast seed

if I am ever to be aware
of the sky when I look up,
the rock when I look down,
and the water when I look across
to take your hand, and in dreaming
shape the land that is both
hidden in your eyes
and escaping from my heart.

Unnatural Selection

the wind should be my religion,
I should know the stone is memory,
be in touch with the water's laughter,
be enchanted with the trees' dreaming,
but I am not a man who lives in nature.
I live in the city. And the city gives a life
the city chooses for me — a parasite,
driving the unnatural,
like the bacteria in my own gut ...
Perhaps that bacteria dares to dream
that it is all that matters, as do I,
who know so much better, living in the city —
but I know something the city does not.

The wind should be my religion,
the stone is memory, the water is laughter,
and sometimes I am enchanted
with the dreaming
of trees ...

while distracted ...

While distracted
I took scissors I did not know I owned
and sheared my calendar,
shredding years, months, weeks, days
even hours thinner then thinner
into streamers, confetti,
tinier and tinier squares,
moments blown by a fierce wind
swirling about me
in patterns, shapes, fancies
I could not discern
until I was hidden
in this cloud of fragmenting white
reaching, groping, grasping
to hold the accelerating blizzard
circling me then shooting away
so quickly I never saw one piece clearly
before another passed it by.

Who's Driving the Hearse?

the voice drones on — awareness fades — I am walking —
walking ... through thin, cool air, my mind stationary
only my feet kick quietly onward,
shiny, black beetle shoes beneath thick grey trousers,
flapping forward momentum, first one leg
then the other, through the leaves —
dry, brown, crisply dead, autumn leaves ...
"Hush," leaves whispering.
I hurry on to some destination
I wish now to remain unknown
"hush, silence, bring only silence to silence — "
Silence (the space between) to silence.
Low, whistling, the wind builds,
stirs the leaves. Gently, first in slow motion
then whirling, flying, streaking, breaking apart,
no longer speaking to me, mute, blinding —
blind ... silent motion carrying me into space —
darkness, who is in control now, who is at the wheel,
wheeling across the vast expanse of — leaves ...
silent, dry, falling.

Bricks and Mirrors

Frolicking to enlightenment,
dancing, singing, hand in hand,
oblivious to all but a single pair of eyes
watching us, through the blue trees,
beneath the emerald sun, all along, all along,
happily convinced there's no God
but oh thank God there's Technicolor,
we laugh; but every yellow brick we travel
leads to a mirror.

Now step cautiously from glass to glass,
we continue, looking only into
one another's eyes. What do we see there?
One frightened, uncertain yearning
reflecting another.

And a voice booms out:
"Bring me the broom of the Wicked Witch
and I'll grant you your heart's desire!"

— but we do not believe him. Anymore.

entropy

— gone too far,
running madly, searching
for an indigo flower
still blooming
in the face of havoc, a chimera
of the undisguised selfish need
to feed our desires.
Daring to think height
will make a difference,
seeking the safety of the rusty bridge
crouching on the last horizon,
aching, we climb,
but cannot move without crying out
— startling swarms of birds,
clouding about us, shrieking,
like tormented gypsy souls
trapped in ice.
Then, before our eyes,
each and every bird
bursts suddenly into fire.
Aghast, staggering back,
we seek comfort in each other
we can no longer give.
Too afraid not to look
we see — we hear — we know.
Swirling anguished cries
rising in pitch
with each flame flaring, then
... cindering out,
falling, silent,
lightless forever.

If ...

just one of those days
when the details of life escape me;
left home with the extension cord
recharging my brain
still plugged into the garage wall,
and something ripped —
                    some connection
somewhere needs repair.
So this is not a day
to try a triple bypass,
or to do anything involving money,
or even to attempt
to cross the street
if there's a button involved
needing a push to stop the traffic,
no, no-o ...
                    Perhaps
this is a day just to write —
but to write of Passions
so sweeping and enormous meaning is transcended,
and the abstract glory of the indefinable
will suddenly illuminate my life
with bright new function and significance!!

If the words will only obey
my absent command.

Not a Morning Person

I stride in anger through the darkness,
alone in social damnation,
cursed to ride the bus
before there is any dawn in the world.
The sun will not show its face
until I accept my fate calmly —
but just enough of a ray
silhouettes a threatening figure.
A goblin rocks back and forth
on a skateboard, lumpy with fashion
that is an accusation of my age.
The kid glares at me, I glare at him,
with a screech from hell
a car pulls out and runs the amber warning;
morning light, on the 7-11 parking lot.

hibiscus

In the sunlit block of unobstructed air
where the hall turns to meet the stairs
there sits the plant; expansive, gravity-defying
greenness. Three stairs up sits the man.
Staring, halted by tender show of affection,
leaves gently stroking his shoulder as he passed.
He envies the slow growth in one place,
no urgency to lose roots nourished by sun,
earth, and water; knowing its world,
focusing inward on outward unfurling;
if left alone, enjoying an endless, natural
lifespan of growth and contemplation.
From his sighs rises the need for action.
Responsibility and resolve remembered, he stands,
runs on. The plant senses his exit.
In unutterable yearning for mobility
it shudders, puts forth one perfect blossom,
white, fragile, touched with rosy moistness,
alive with beauty only when briefly noted
by eyes passing by often too quickly to care.

herbs afoot

a brushfire of yabbering idiots,
the plants uproot themselves
to dance away the night
intoxicated on vigaro
and air too rich to breathe;
a drunken greenery of revels.
They do not wish us to suspect
they own the gift of mobile glee,
wisely reserving motion
only for moments of joy.
Would humans,
in their own good thyme,
only act as sagely.

mutter, mutter

not understanding
the gravity of the situation
the idle thinker
let go his head
which swiftly
drifted away

* * *

the actor
looked out at the prairie
and said:
"i was in a show like that
once. someone stole
the scenery
and never put it
back."

* * *

i like
to sit on a rock
and read
on a hot summer day,
one toe
dangling
in the silent stream

* * *

the oversensitive woman
likes to sit
in a soundproof room
and listen to
dreams
of different sorts of apes

* * *

her life is
a river
with strong currents
not knowing
which way to flow

* * *

apparently
there was a chest
of masks upstairs,
but he didn't
own a key

* * *

"heroes are too noisy,"
she told him,
"i prefer the silent,
sinister type."
this upset his composure
but did give him hope

* * *

a caring mother
of monsters and poets,
she deserved longer joy
of her children
with golden hair
and innocent hearts

* * *

there were
pictures of jesters
in his house
because
he liked
their smiles

* * *

"i don't think
people
go to enough weddings,"
she observed.
"they're too busy
with funerals,"
he replied.
so she hit him

* * *

in the circumstances
he would have liked
to have run to the king
but
they hadn't seen one
in ages

* * *

she drew hearts and arrows,
he drew numbers.
she said "you don't love me"
he counted the hearts
and said
"i didn't count the arrows.
are we communicating
yet?"

* * *

in every diamond
there is a flaw,
she meant to say,
but he preferred
the way
she got it backwards

* * *

she liked to think
that if a bird
fell in the water,
a fish
would teach him
how to swim
but
she had her doubts
about the bird
teaching the fish
to fly

* * *

it would be easy
to fly
if words
were light

* * *

i don't understand
what i'm doing,
but i don't think
that means
i shouldn't have
a good time

* * *

i puzzled out your beauty
on a Monday afternoon
as there's nothing else of consequence
in all my world and soul

Iron in the Broccoli

deciding the answer to his problem
was to provide a movie-soundtrack for his life
he chose "Conan the Barbarian"
because when the choir thunders
Crom's fury
you can't understand the language
and he could just as easily substitute
"Now-I'm-going-to-thegrocerystore!
Where-I'll-chop-the-heads-off-alltheparcelboys!
And-ravish-the-fair-checkout
ma-a-i-id-dddens-s-s!"

There was a sale on veggies, too.

Employment Opportunity

Not getting what I want out of life
I've posted notice: Wanted — Harpooneer,
to walk before me, barbed steel ready to throw
on a moment's notice, target: what I need,
what I want, what I lust for —
a day without my damned disease,
energy and opportunity
for passions both secret and profound,
freedom from fatigue turning my guts to water,
the vitality to smile even when I don't want to,
and a little cash wouldn't run amiss either.
Applicant must have ready aim and true,
so at the slightest hint of prey I can yell
"Throw, my spearman, throw and reel 'er in;
with a strong back and barbed steel
we'll change my life tonight!"

The Long Sky

The land without walls made him nervous,
all that blue pouring down and flowing out.
He felt threatened, whisked away, a speck insignificant
against an expanse too broad
to fit anywhere but the prairie.

So he tied cruel steel hooks to his hands, to his feet,
and he lay spread-eagled, full-bodied across the sod,
digging in; for fear the clouds envied him his gravity.
But he forgot to tie down his forehead.

The sky yanked his eyes back
filling his vision with too much light.
As the sun rose, hooks or no hooks,
he was away.

The little boy sighed,
too late to tie his string
to that disappearing foot —
the man made such a beautiful kite.

sunrise

Morning on the Arlington Street Bridge
seen from the corner of my eye,
a Philly Joe flick driving the beat
of the drive to work.
Old metal, black bars caging in the rat race;
a mad flock, birds desperately swirling
through, above, almost always away from the prison,
but never quite;
the sun rising golden
beneath the red then blue sky
above the gray, rusting tracks,
more old metal, more bars
steel veins aching to infinity.

But Miles on the CD
focuses on the urban jazz moment
drawing the crossing lines
of force and old metal
despite it all
into the beauty of the day —

the shadow of birds
                        beyond the bars
            soaring against the sun.

Catch the Drift

Some people read the world
like I read books;
recognize when it's spring
before I realize
I've missed it again;
know when summer's happening
without having to think about it
afterwards;
catch the drift
the first time.

Good thing I have a child
to teach me
there are seasons.

A Middle Earth Memory

The lake lay huge and blue in its simple affection.
Rock, sand, and every delightful sky
a true fellowship,
every watching, breathing tree
welcomed him, took him to their heart.
His feet never touched the ground
and a land came to life.
A stick for a sword
in sight of all that gave living,
the green, the yellow and red, the blue,
his parents dropped him there.
As he slammed the car door behind him
his delight was utter and complete.
He was a small enough boy
no lie was insurmountable.
In that perfect time
he ran the roads of high adventure;
no matter how grave the danger
no black rider could catch him
in the autumn of the world.
Living the greatest book he knew to be
the heroes triumphed. And he was among them.
His soul was lifted into memory
and his ghosts could play.

Nature was freed to be part of him
as he flew on the wind like the waves.

The Spinning Tree

If all the universe is supported by one tree
then understand this — each root, each twig
is in motion. Each branch, each limb,
each bough, all moving independently and
finally the trunk, rotating at such a speed
its meaning will never be understood.

But each root and twig that touches another
changes that movement touched by touch,
and everyone spins off in new directions again.

And each root and twig *will* try to touch another ...

We must rescue the mad sisters,
vainly trying to measure each man's life
with increasingly careless snips of the shears.
We must lower a hand and haul them up
upon this tree, then wind their threads
about the trunk and watch in delight
as the threads spray off into space
each a brilliant, shining color of its own.
We'll catch the ends and fly,
still in motion, always trying to touch,
to keep the spin alive in movement
we haven't even yet dared to dream.

Hand in hand the sisters will dance
across the rainbow bridge to the end of time,
and smash the scissors that snipped the threads
and never, never, never
                    come to rest ...

The Thunder of Leaves

when trees flow like water, they stream so slow
we do not suspect their shape-taking whisper
to be the path of least resistance to the sky

i enter their dark ocean without a sound
amid the rippling wind the shadows sigh
i hear the memory of hushed and ancient rain

sometime, when lying in the waterfall of green
i long to be deafened
by the thunder

of leaves

soon after, we found ourselves yearning to live a luscious bravo life,
surrounded by our expectations made flesh, a picaresque tale
with no ending and we, as the immortal heroes, always finding
perfect love in the final reel, the perfect kiss, the enduring walk
on the beach in the dying sunlight, the end of the restless urges
driving us on to our own distraction, eternally beyond our understanding.
But the Thieves Circus fell upon us instead, kidnapping our best intentions,
and holding them for ransom against a fortune we would never inherit.
And that was when we learned to build our love with only
our most bitter illusions, if we were to know any treasure at all.

My Disappointment With the Moon

There came a time I claimed my heart was ruled by the moon
for all lunatic emotions should be governed by mystery,
pale reflected light

and distance.

But no.
It's all a joke of the wind.
A not-so-celestial body too precisely placed
to moderate the turbulence of worlds within
as well as the world's without;
an afterallempty orb,
pulling on tides of sea and air, not shadowy mysteries of love,
not full after all with the emotion we fear to acknowledge within
and so cast high and away as far as we can see;

just

further evidence
of a carefully

contrived universe uncaring

of a man living by pale light and distance
misdirecting touch and vision
without from within.

He who mourns his love by the moon
measures only the distance
between life on this planet
and his heart.

Fire Lake

the dark green line rounds the lake,
accepts the sunset, flames leap upon the water
and upon his rock.

"Somewhere in this universe
there *must* be a woman
with my eyes in her heart!"

waters gently lap,
calmed
by the sun's dying inferno

throbbing quiet at the end of the world.
There is life in the pines,
he drifts among them like a ghost
unable to make touch manifest.

he burns, as the lake itself burns,
shedding clothing and reason,
plunging off the rock.

water will not quench his passion
anymore than the lake reflects the sunset.

he swims into the fire.

In the Late Afternoon

In that time in the late afternoon
by water shooting blinding arcs of gold
romping in green grass all she wore
seemed made of sunshine
and I learned delight in body, in smile
almost set free;
but I could not speak,
remained grimly silent,
I could not say to her
this is what I've learned.
And so the moment died,
learning for both of us ending before it began.
Yet there is such necessity in that moment;
every boy should be able to speak once
especially to she who is not certain of this truth,
that in those moments of the late afternoon
with blue water blinding gold against the green grass
and skin touched only by sunshine
you are pretty, you are delight,
you fill my heart;
then instead of tongue-tied arrogance
and smiles lost in dust-filled shyness
we would all be beautiful.

The Ghost Across the Hall

She whispers to me,
"I press your body with my soul,"
and love is a summer scent
as teardrops open time.
She haunts the clock across the hall.
I seek her when the sun is high.
I never quite see her — but —
the shadow of the last note
she sang pierces my eyes,
pierces my mind, my heart.
Arms outstretched, embracing all
she flows across the floor.
Her ghost haunts my daylight
as her reality never did in life.

Ophelia Rises

Asleep without reason
on a damp bed of roses,
crystal water
and white lilies her shroud,
does she float
in acceptance and beauty
through the undiscovered country;
does she dream?

And in her dream,
does she sing
the unanswered melody
of a prince never to be king,
never realizing
into harmony
of her making
or any other's?

What new harmony
does she realize then,
lost only
in the endless rhythm
of damp roses.

Into The Pool Of —

Time. Not here. Elsewhere.

Movement. The fugitive dreamer
on the lam from heat and light
leaping over the bones of trees
scattered across the sand,
headed for the mountain,
for treasure to be shared
lying beyond the strictly skeletal.

Heat. Blinding.
Light. Incinerating.
Death. Must be fled. You must flee
over the mountain, then —
                          falling,

surprised, into a space
only primeval man knew.
You arrive. At a private place
you could not know the mountain hid.

Shelter. You slide naked
into the water, into the pool,
keeping your hand on the warm rock
to keep your head afloat
as your body is reclaimed.
The water is deep. There is no bottom.
The fugitive knows sanctuary at last.

Privacy. In which a stranger
seeks you. She knows, she must do this too.
In moments, she slides naked beside you,
into the pool, into your arms.

Ecstacy, drowning.
In a deep, kiss-locked embrace
as you abandon breath
you sink into the bottomless deep,
the pool closing over your heads.
Now there is no surface,
just as there is no bottom,
just two suspended in a stranger's kiss,
pooling dim necessity.

Thea's Canyon

Enduring this present focused only
on tomorrow, needing the long, slow
silent contemplation of now, with faith
devoted only to water, I flow to the canyon
painted in her heart.

So much to be fled, meaning so little,
the certain violation of the senses;
she seeks the necessary desert,
arid nothing wherein sense and sensibility
experience so little, so much.

And in this heat at the center of all,
lies the pool where she bathes ...

Privacy not to be violated, but in this moment
her nakedness is not private. She is a vessel,
as am I, holding her, awakening,
skin to slippery skin, no voice,
only song, nothing to be heard,
only singing.

and then ...

she moves, ink flowing in the night

a dry leaf rustles, no twig snaps.
evening air settles beneath the heavy scent
of jasmine; so the music plays,
improvising upon a theme
                                        first a flute
then a crying, muted cornet ... I hide.

Beneath the pines, needles prickling warm comfort,
I wait. Beyond the music, a smooth ripple
in syncopated, illogical rhythm. She descends.
No mystery, no menace, only delight.

ninja in squeaky shoes

choices

as we struggle upward
in sanctifying shadow of trees
the procession drums down the hill
carrying torches and cruel intent
in clear and present urgency;
goodness for all, enforced as necessary.
Our eyes meet. "I'm cold," you tell me,
needing more than answers.
Chilled by the torches' passing,
where trees and path meet
we choose the trees.
We find the way beneath
the lower branches — into stillness.
Piny blackness, sap running, not stultified,
dry, needling wisdom. We huddle.
I light a small lamp, shielding the flame
from outside prying and our fragile shelter.
In its glow, we embrace,
our kisses warm and secure
as the old-growth forest itself.
We grow tall in our tenderness,
as the torch-bearers
sink deeper, ever deeper
into mists
of bitter regret.

scintilla

shimmer in the park,
just beyond the iron gate,
darting beneath the pines
leading on a thought
fleeting beyond the moment;
more, yes, there is more,
delight, race into the dark,
must catch that thought,
that moment, that joy;
then just as quickly gone —
disappearing, shrinking
on the edge of darkness,
laughing into mystery.
A second rapid needling,
light and fire —
never seen again.
Except in the memory
of your eyes.

Physics

somewhere you dance alone;
breezy, transparent gossamer caressing
your lightly skipping form
as I would, softly,
with great expression;
you move — defy gravity,
your body soaring
at one with spirit,
lifting — no force attaching you
to any mass,
and therein lies my desire
to alter the motion
of the universe.

Godiva Night

Last seen beneath blonde moonlight
running the green broadsoul
we wore only words
as we rode proud horses
to temptation and beyond.
No one dared speak
as each image we wrote
bared only what we chose,
never what truly mattered.
"Let them use their imaginations!"
we cried when we stripped to ride
and to rob and to ravage,
to write our energy beneath the stars
on this Lady Godiva Night,
when we strew no garment in protest,
only in faith we can fashion
each other and the world.

But just before we disappeared
we turned and stared, each at the other;
we listened — we tried to truly hear
what the other spoke only
in the naked moment between ourselves.
And we saw —

      no images,
            just a man, a woman
               in love, alive,
          capable of clothing each day
          in what the other wants to hear,
          what we truly wish to say,
          what we truly wish to show   each other,
             naked and forever.

we whisper the wind
      and murmur of memory
and finally know only
      the look and the wordless devotion
      that opens us each to the other
      eternally,
      beneath the blonde moonlight
running naked
      across the green broadsoul ...

Cooling Down, Just

A different impetus arises,
you must not cut your hair,
you must never cut your hair,
I give you words of beauty
to express your dream, my fee
so you will not cut your hair.
In gratitude, you do not consider hair,
offering kind words instead,
a heart surprisingly open,
breeding appreciation and respect,
quiet desire moving our lips
together gently, seeking tenderness
not release.

Subtly, we touch, and do not lust,
do not lust, but seek touch;
warm knowledge of each other
caresses our psyches; we shiver,
together. I move my lips to
dryly brush your hair, inhaling
your calm beauty, knowing yes,
here there is peace ... you lean
your head in comfort on my shoulder,
one moment of silence held,
no promise, no demand,
equal and content.

the signal

When the rain stopped, it was late;
too late to sleep. Rising from the bed
in the grey room; silent, naked feet move
cautiously to the window, the open window.
Eyes centered by huge pools of black
stare out at the street light,
whipped into fearful animation by lashing branches,
shadows of snatching black fingers
of bone and malice. Still there is no sound.
He looks beyond the trees,
beyond the light, beyond the rain, the street,
beyond all the obstacles keeping them apart
and calls out the one sound he wants her to hear.
A huge, plum-red poppy, velvety petals
alive and moist with a thin sheen of pearldropping
rain, goes probing through the night,
soon lost to his sight. But the sound finds her.
Half a city away, walking on a different street,
a different land of the mind,
where there is sound, there are lights,
there is yelling and cursing and laughter
and life. And in the midst of this tumult
the poppy descends upon her and she hears.
Overcome, grasping at her body, she races
to a dimlit alley, alone, somewhere private.
The poppy courses through her, the redness,
the velvet, the moist, deep emotion, wave after wave
of vibration rippling her body, building,
until she falls back, aching, against the wall
and the flower blooms through. Breathless, she sinks,
slowly, to the ground, in utter satisfaction,
knowing she is loved. She has heard.

Again, the rain begins to fall ...

If you're grinning ...

If you're grinning when you get back
then I'll know

how voyages with joyous intent
end in unexpected places;
how you couldn't learn to fly
but discovered a healthy sense of gliding;
how even rained on circuses
are sources of color and light;
how you found a warm, dry place
to lay your head in nature;
how swimming in unforeseen pools
leads to unforeseen delights;
how dark eyes and warm hands
are necessary;
how a kiss doesn't have to end
until another begins;
how needs and desires
should both be met;
how searches for beauty
always lead finally deep within;
how every poem about you
doesn't have to end in song;
but most of all
how you know now
I truly loved you all along.

to breathe in a hostile climate

green black shards oppressing
filling the space between us,
heat so swampy, tendrils dragging down,
down into fever claustrophobic no air
that doesn't burn, we are lost,
we are lost, alone, apart, hands reaching,
yearning through wet and filthy particles
fingers touching, clutching, caressing
pull, pull, out of the mud together,
grasp and hold, body to body
but still no air, lungs collapsing
the swamp is rising, the trees are falling
the green black shards piercing
knives in our chests, hold, hold,
now, the only way to breathe
your lips on mine, my lips on yours,
the only way to breathe
in a hostile climate
one long, encompassing ...
                              relaxing ...
                                      arousing ...

kiss.

Twice the Speed of Roses

What remains, what still grows,
and at what speed
so long after the seed was planted,
bloomed and seemingly
returned to earth?

Red, ever more intensely rich in meaning
as the reality passes
in a sniff of scent
enveloping every sense that matters
when I think of you ...

familiar song

when first
      the flower of your beauty bloomed for me
and we discovered
      the sanctity of touch I knew you like the enchantment
of music
      heard with senses attuned to the deeper flow
      of meaning
      but we mustn't —
               no —
         do not —
            listen too closely.
            we lose ourselves.
            we lose track
                of our better senses
            in our for-everyday
                hearing,
        in details that do not matter; thin weeds
           of dischord
       blight the green yearning
               of our harmony.

     better not
        to pay such close attention,
all music
        grows familiar in time
        if the beauty
        we raise to the surface
           in each other
        is as truly irresistable
        as we know
        it must be.

Then close your eyes and listen.
        hear

                      the soft rain
            your
            crimson petals
                        drifting
                down
            upon
        my naked body
        i overflow

            no longer caring
                    where i
    end
        and you   begin.

Heartscape with Water

Beside the setting sunlight
on the naked bodies,
a boy plays in the sand.
Love is shed there, blood rushing,
lapping quietly against the current.
Sunset brings loss, but the boy,
seeming a ghost to the lovers
cannot be touched.

It does not matter who they are,
identity is not important;
a woman, stretching like a young girl
blooming as a flower upon the wall
carries all of greenness, all the wild,
all nature within a budding grove.

All of this, so gentle,
so romantic, is not lost.
All is well and joyous.
Dreamt of so sweetly
there and there again
is a girl perhaps not perfect,
quiet in the early evening.
She is pretty, and I arise,
enfused with the vibrant sky.

Inevitably,
the boy becomes her lover,
with all my heart believing
when all the land that matters
is a mountain to run down
there is no beauty
that is not desire for life.

how long did I wait here, supporting my friend as a crutch,
staring upwards as tears left streaks in the grime
beneath eyes unwilling to focus upon his reality or my own?
This is the path where we chose to dance with the wrong women,
not realizing they were emanations of a dread female presence
that had instead chosen us as the unlikely recipients of her favour.
Neither of us will know the music long enough to hear our own
final kiss, to stagger the last few inches of the stately gavotte
waltzing us into the grave slowly being dug for us
since the moment we were born. And what knowledge do we
leave with from this dance? After the last cadence fades,
will we finally know our partner, and realize what she demands.

The catherine wheel

opening up, looking back, spinning the wheel
is chaining yourself naked
not entirely between the spikes,
hooking your eyes and heart open
as the fireworks begin to explode
electric sparking daggers too close
to body, heart, and eyes;
and then the rotation starts ...

Slowly at first, then building speed,
until you reach a blinding velocity
but still your eyes and heart are hooked open
and fire sparks in blazing sheets
and all of you is burnt within from without
and without from within until you lock —
                  hold yourself rigid in just one place
and the catherine wheel rips free,
slashing you as it goes spinning outward,
spinning wider, wider into space
until it cannot touch you
but still you are its center
and still its light burns bright
for all to see
          as you collapse
              now blinded
                    by just your tears ...

Kids in Circles

Spinning from one age to another
I'm wilfully bat-blind
to the weight keeping me in motion
but not moving on,
dizzy in one spot only.
However, only kids ask questions
as embarrassing as yours.
So when I reel for a moment
just as a child, alone again,
not understanding,
not sharing in something
I shouldn't have to look for,
lost and afraid
in the tall unfriendly forest
I grew up in,
where I was never welcome,
I see the friend I never had
the same age as me,
and we run off to find the answers.
Inquisitive and innocent,
poking at shadows
in a maze full of circles
I lead us to the center
full of black screens.
We must see what lies behind!
Knowing something I don't,
you hold back and let me
lift the first screen.
Straining and gasping under weight
too heavy for little arms and sensibilities,
I mutter "Go ahead — look."
Hearing the right cue,
knowing you're not really a child
and neither am I,
you spin me again:
"No. You look."

Giving Up Control

is throwing myself off a cliff into darkness,
no bottom in sight, wearing forty parachutes,
some with ropes so thick I've been weaving them
since I was born and then cutting, one after another,
each and every line until I dangle from just
one single thread, picking up speed, and before
cutting the last line, wondering: How, just how
will anyone catch me now? from below, from above?

and not knowing the answer
but cutting the line anyway.

In the Face of the Morning News

lilacs blooming at the end of May

full past fullness
my evening walk, after supper,
the usual route
sun shining, young girls
playing baseball
old folks waiting for the bus
just outside the church
all along the route
not a leaf out of place
and just before turning,
a mother and young son
sitting on a fence
outside the 7 Eleven
laughing, happy

— me, too,
bravely out and home again,
proving it's all still real
(First thing I heard —
late last night,
19 year old fatally stabbed
four blocks west
16 year old beaten to death
three blocks east)

lilacs blooming at the end of May.

one puzzle, many pieces, no clues

should the flowers not bloom
while children are dying
should we not weep?

must children not die
because flowers are blooming
should we not weep?

should we not weep
flowers are blooming
children don't care

Owl

i.

Eagerness for mutual consent lying in our gaze
abruptly vanishes — I recognize with shock
there can be no commonground between man's eyes
and a bird's. You watch me, still, eyes wide,
huge, round, yellow, with piercing black centers.
I know now. You writhe backwards, arms, breasts
twisting, transforming, an explosion of feathers
into flight — the sheets of the bed torn,
my body clawed, blood on skin and white silk.
The woman brought me to the bed — but the owl departs.
What did her passion take from me?
Why was I hunted — memory strikes like a spear.
Her eyes. Just before the change.
There can be no understanding.

ii.

Outward wounds healed, I walk again
beneath grey skies and buildings, contemplating
loss and commitment — could I commit
to that savage grace, would I endure?
The flame burnt hot but not brightly,
fusing our bodies together to prey on each other
without remorse, regret, ignoring barriers
real and imagined ... Much silence is needed
afterwards, body immobile, restoring, remembering.
Watching. For the next prey?
My attention pivots, wrenched upwards.
At the top corner of the building — a stone owl.
Not a gargoyle, not a living bird — an idol.
To worship. To warn. Others have known the fear
of being locked beneath her gaze. Others have fled.

iii.

With silken caress, long feathers brush my neck.
I turn again — face her, in human guise.
She is pleased. She is smiling. She accepts
my uncertain tribute. She knows more than I,
and does not share — kisses me instead, nails
arching, pulling at the skin on my neck, but not
piercing, letting me know — she casts her cloak
about me and I am yanked, flying, into the night,
never expecting, lost in the mystery
plucking me at will from a life I dared
believe routine. Dropped, unsupported,
just as abruptly — thrashing, flailing down,
out of control, panicked — as she prefers.
All the easier to take at will. I crash.
Body miraculously not broken. This time.

iv.

But she allows me one truth.
Despite her terror, I did not flee.
I do not always fear.
She does not admit equality, but ...
She does respect.

Which will not save my life,
but nourishes my soul.

The Buddha Pool

Too much flak; the noise, the dull blades of no consequence,
the unrelenting sour smell of aimless discontent
drive me back from the city, to the low ground
deep in the forest, beyond the great stones to the pool.
There are many there already, not relating.
Leaving the strife in midstride we arrive
in all manner of dress, suits, ties now discarded,
rolled up jeans, shorts, short skirts, long skirts held high
we wade through the ankle deep water
too murky to reflect but soothing.
I remove socks, shoes, roll up cuffs, ease into the coolness,
I move my feet against the insolent resistance
that links us all and try to think. In the pool,
the only woman who meets my eyes is singing.
All others still blindly carry anger in their eyes,
but she denies hers in song: there is great emotion
in her melody, her voice paints a better world
than we can hope to live in. Our eyes meet,
I smile, but I am not complicit in her song.
Stabbing the sore tooth of my pain, I hug her body to mine,
to keep the water, our souls, and the depths of love
and struggle fierce within us still in motion.

The Specialist

The counselor calls me back,
unable to reach her client
who speaks now only in dreams.
I set up: the patient, asleep,
draped across the chair
behind me playing quietly
at the piano, the mirror
in front of all.
I stare into my eyes.
They become doors. They open.
Both of me enter —
I emerge into fresh sun and bright air,
each inhalation drawing me to hallucination,
the landscape every colour of the music,
filled with the singing of her perception,
each shifting, breathing, beautiful tableau

— and above it all she flies.
I drop to my knees, close to the green,
yearning in envy, but my feet
could never leave her ground.
My despair reaches out, drags,
brings her plummeting to earth.

In sorrow, I assume my task completed.
But she finds me where I kneel,
staring down into the darkening grass.
She consoles me, reassures me,
it is no sin not to be able to fly.

Tenderly she kisses me;
we fall
        falling ...
                falling —

The music stops. She awakes.
I do not.

Charlie Parker

junkies shooting different rhythm
black sheep aristocracy
the strangest people
loved Charlie Parker
and one of them was me

Charlie Parker died
in New York City
and everyone insists
it must be tragically

Yardbird Parker died
in New York City
the only ones laughing
were him and me

Bird died watching television
no saxophone in hand
no saxophone in heart nor mind
a juggler set him laughing
Charlie Parker, he died laughing,
laughing not alone.

the jazzman in the Dutch window

i.

Chet sat in the windowsill
melancholy night tunes floating
from his mind, his lips, his groin
he didn't know anymore
where the sound came from
or where it went.
Realized with mild amusement
his reason for living, his soul in music
was no longer tethered to this life
"I left the world today," he laughed.
He leaned forward, wondering
how far he could go
before something or somebody
said "Stop." and then realized
with tremendous glee
no one ever would —
          he's still falling. Always was.

ii.

There is an old man
with a broom
standing on a wide cement patio
somewhere in Asia
looking over a garden
staring at the breeze
and the vital green
perfectly sculpted
but always one weed away
from chaos,
thinking: why should I ever move again?

Running Through Glass

Putting myself in mind of the past to look forward
I come to the window — I'm stalled.
I'm there, I hurt, the same,
but do I really remember or just ache anew?
I must look with the eyes I had then,
see what I saw once and make the halted light
clock forward — I come to the window.

The old window, big as me then,
looking out on so much green
and the road, barren, empty, dusty ...
The green still lies beyond.
The frame is worn,
round in spots and grey with age,
smooth to run my hand over,
full of character and spleen; I see —
the window. I see the window very clearly, but
looking out now as I did then I still do not see —

Suddenly. Not to see. To feel.

Only then do I presume perception
through a window out of time
and know there can be movement taken
more fair than any still memory
and the road itself is not so intriguing
as the dust lingering upon it, rising, descending,
in hazy image anything but still
rushing onwards towards the green.

And I see now, exactly what I saw then
not knowing mirrors from windows.
I see myself, escaping, running in the road
to the green beyond knowing there has to be
something better, and from this vantage point
four decades later on paper I wave goodbye,
good luck, and see through the window
what I always knew —

                    I'm far too preoccupied

to wave back.

— But oh, the glorious light!

On The Borderline

"Oh, I'm fine."
Relief —
and I cannot pretend;
I try but I lie,
lost in the limbo
not the disease —
regardless, I'm not well.

I am sick; "no, I'm fine";
I do not breathe, I only live,
stumbling on exhausted,
so little to stir me —
I've dropped my standard.

I've just got into the habit
crushed beneath the burden
of doing anything worth doing;
not enough, not enough,
but still I protest —

"How are you?"
I am not unwell.
No primary symptoms today,
on the borderline.

The Visit

still strangely separate, I watched,
unfamiliar with the scene,
with the character playing the title role
in an utterly normal day, healthy,
playing with his child, sharing tender,
quiet moments with his wife, no
absolute worries about money, no fear
of time and all its whirling stresses
and I suddenly realized — oh. That's me.
The me I ... dimly remember ...
Oh, yes —

                   the way life used to be,
never phoned, never wrote, but finally
came to visit.

What I Fear

Stamped fragile
so often, so hard
I am broken
and leaking.

Still I fear
this is really nothing;
I say this is really nothing;
there are days
I believe
this is really nothing.

I fear
I play on your sympathy
for nothing.
I've grown so used to the attention.
Lying down when I want to.

Forgetting
that I need to.

Sunrose

Carrying sadness ...
conscience echoing ...
holes in each arm
digging for *this* disease
or that ...
under gray skies,
I don't anticipate
the freshness of flowers
will bloom again
in my countenance;
when surprised
by a strange, pale pink sunset
I must wonder ...

how does this light
reflect from my face?

traveling wrongward

Beyond the moment of sudden discovery,
beyond perception,
in the secret place
that is not secret
but openly judged by others,
I straddle flesh and nakedness
and sweat in the swampy heat
embracing the sin of misdirection,
following the dwindling river
into the wet murk,
through green filament trees,
piercing needles of shadow
a ceiling between the thin sun
and my body.
The great water recedes
in my memory, whispering:
"she is not here, this is not home,
these are only ghosts, exquisitely within ... "

And the river feeds me
to the dagger of gloom.

The Thirteenth

Driven from the scene,
chased again from the light
that should be shared,
by babbling nonentities
with stakes in their hearts
and the paranoid desire
to drive one deep into mine, I retreat,
blend back into the shadow
that is not the shadow of the shadow
but the shadow itself,
a yearning component
of the silhouette, the monolith
hanging imponderable
over the trees moved by a hissing wind
chanting truth
in a halfheard rustle.
The mob withers, gives up the chase,
unable to face even a hint
of their own empty whispering.
They fall back, I fall forward,
needing to rejuvenate
before struggling to struggle again.
I slide between shadows
to the pool of ancient sorrows,
where the chanting
becomes a wail.
The water shimmers ...

Guardian spirits now smoke, now light,
now flesh, rising luminous then plunging madly
splashing nightmare
overrunning the waking world —
sense my presence.
Halt their play.
Cry out their delight,
welcome me back.
I wade willingly naked
into the pool.
Slowly, joyful, singing
they drag me under ...

"back, back to wailing
heart beating, beat,
the cry of sustaining light
away, away from the ugly day,
slowly, down, beat, down,
know the quiet joy, let go
let them go
we let you go
... now."

Deep. Deeper.

Deepest.

Detachable Unit

The first step was easy,
he found the latch
and detached his brain from his heart.
It wasn't much of a search
to find the next latch,
mouth from brain.
Then, in quick succession:
his needs from any other needs,
his comfort from his environment,
himself from all other people.
Then, after an intensive, grueling,
fully committed search, all he was from

the entire world.

In the garden on Old Oak Island
the crewman lifts his shovel like a shroud.
"Bury the treasure," his Captain orders.
We know he's digging his own grave.
When he's dead, the Captain will
sprinkle salt and water over his body,
so he will not grow into a tree.

Ereshkigal, my companion

i.

I do not wish to own this mystery.
Staggering disoriented, the focus
of unwanted attention; unfurling layers
of hate, and yearning; of love,
life and death; such beauty
aching and alluring, such loss
devastating and final.
I love this woman of piercing light,
this being and this state of being
calling to me from the darkness,
binding my heart with silken veil,
delicately caressing each searing nerve
with unconditional emotion,
reminding me,
as long as I am here or anywhere
she is with me,
questioning the essence of my soul.

ii.

A vast, unruffled expanse tempts me,
stops me to watch. Winds skim the powdery surface,
sand shifts, a high-pitched reed begins to wail.
With lyric undulation the sand parts like the sea.
The remains of antiquity arise, rough, grit-rounded
out of recognition. All that's left of a civilization
that could not conceive of its own ending.
Echoing off ancient stars, the music continues.
She emerges like a fountain from the sand,
belly bare, eyes accusing and inviting, painted toes
with bells, hands weaving light to bedazzle
my shadowed eyes; she dances, hips, torso, arms
gyrating to connect me to what is most untrustworthy
within me. Inviting me, saying yes, I am interested
in you … She draws me from my chair, across the desert,
as one veil strips away after another.
She takes my hand and with the other
casts back the tombstone from the grave like a bedcover,
drawing me down, overwhelming my consent,
into the one embrace she still trusts.

iii.

Casting her last veil across my eyes, she convinces me
I am indeed the lover I imagine myself to be.
Pumping union of flesh, smooth, slick, probing, testing,
clutching, embracing, enchanting as necessary,
giving pleasure before taking it, the fuse
filling her with molten, glowing flame.
We cascade, a waterfall of ecstacy in mutual delight.
She pools, thighs, breasts, lips liquefying, engulfing me;
she seeks to drown me in the warm wet. Ebbing, flowing,
overwhelming tidal passion, offering no opportunity to breathe,
in moments I am lost, irrevocable, until the climax,
when I arise howling, wolf, not man; the curse
of loving a stranger. Like the moon, she rises,
shining, pale, gentle and proprietorial
of her worshipping beast.

iv.

Ripping the veil from my animal senses
she shows me not flesh, but bones; bones
surrounding, tumbling, avalanching upon us
from all sides, filling our bed.
As the man wolf I sweep her from the grave,
leap to cooler, fresher air, armouring her sudden frailty.
I hold her, seeking not to crush, but
tenderly to support; she weeps.
Why? "These are the bones of your children."
My strength departs, I sink to my knees,
to comprehend this grief
I must be only human.

V.

She grows alien, expression no longer recognizable,
eyes glazed, spread wide in appalled terror
of what is not without, but within. She shakes me,
shrieking she has been violated, her blood is on my hands,
there is death in the world and her life is now in death,
there can be no hope, only loud, violent despair ...
Denying my own tears, I wait, and focus,
try to find the calm in turbulent waters.
Frenzy wears thin, her strength fails;
I am released, free to act from my own will.
Still, I hold her; I hold her still.
Until she accepts my attention. I embrace her. I know.
In the horror, in the death, we can only hold each other closer.
Both renewed in value, she is abruptly small, human.
Vulnerable. Thin, with long hair and sad smile.
Our eyes meet.

And therein, still lies the mystery.

I've seen the angry dead roll by me at six in the morning
a rack of hills and valleys of pain
and seen the wave fill the vacuum left behind
with a profoundly disturbing emptiness of wonder,
wondering why, what was the point,
why lay down in hate and let the nearest engine of rage
drive over you, why, how can I comprehend such a lack of reason
for if there is no reason for an action
how can there be action taken; yet the will was there,
and no one can even say truly for how long,
the desire to end it all in misery, the misery
that was all that was left to be known.
Every expectation if expectations were even allowed,
shattered.

And I didn't even have to say to myself,
that is not me. Even if it takes the rest of my life
to know why.

Crow

Don't, crow, don't follow me so,
don't fill my day with thoughts of woe,
don't mourn so loud from in your tree,
mourning so loud as mourning can be,
don't, crow, leave my mourning be.

Fly, crow, fly into the sky,
grey as the blue is usually high,
fly, crow, fly black as the night,
take this grey and this mourning
from out of my sight.

Sing, crow, sing as you fly,
don't tell me of clouds so grey in the sky,
sing in a voice untouched by woe;
I cannot bear to weep so low,
I cannot bear to hear you, crow.

Weep, crow, weep if you must,
what crows do and men do
must fall into dust.

life without oceans

... i've never seen an ocean.

     perhaps they're just a rumour
        like a belief
           in my own vulnerability.
           Vast, mapless,
           waves threatening to drown me whole;
               powerful, powerful
rumours ...

No. I doubt there can be such things.
     Until I fall in,
     drowning in what I don't believe in
         until I must believe
         to be saved,
         utterly saved by what is
         dark, blue, alive, wonderful,
         never to be taken for granted
         or ever, ever doubted ...

heading south, we fell in with a disreputable band
of Peruvian bookherders, certainly not above the odd job
of rustling. When the conquistadorial militia fell upon us
like pelting rain on the wrong side of the mountain,
we took shelter in the last cave beyond sanctuary. Our hosts
told us of the unruly bands of the wild unpublished they keep on
a hidden plateau in the Andes, writings considered unfit to print
in any language, the great stories that do not fit
the market's perception of what a book should and must be,
and never will. And they feared — if they did not return in time,
would these volumes of necessity find a way out of the mountains?

Spring Dream

Eight months. Absolute, stupefying,
petrifying winter boredom ...
immobile. At my desk. No one notices. Or cares.

Spring sunshine. Trying to pour through the filthy window.
Doesn't revive me. Revives a fly. Starts crawling up my window.
Slowly. Slowly. Slow ... My eyes don't move to follow it.

CBC Two shuts someone's eyes. Out of the blue — fiddle music

(A vision. Middle of the night. Staring at a footbridge,
crossing a river into absolute blackness. Lanterns on the bridge
arching away into the rich dark. The fiddle picks up tempo.
Sounds. Laughter. Bare feet pattering. Dancing.
Many coloured demons,
wood nymphs, silky water sylphs in skimpy gossamer,
fauns, centaurs, angels, monsters, maidens,
dancing, leaping, bounding,
the fiddle saws faster, body swept away by the mob's delight,
onto the bridge, across the bridge, away, away, alive —)

fly's half-way up the window

(vision blurring, all colour and delight, happy, bouncing bodies
and body parts pressing around, touching, provoking,
hands in glee lifting, elevating —)

three-quarters

(shooting out in joy the length of a football field —)

hits the top. Fly grows gigantic, horrible buzzing, chainsaws into action,
swoops down, six hairy legs grab me, carry me away screaming —
(who's dreaming now?)

Spring. Watch your back.

Three Variations on an Icon:
Blackbeard's Flag

i.

picture this —

upon a field of black,
a white skeleton stands,
in his right hand,
he holds an hour glass,
in his left a spear
piercing a red heart
with three red blood-drops
falling

ii.

What was he *on*?
Bloodshot eyes,
beard up to just below 'em
down again to his waist,
always carrying six pistols,
a cutlass in his teeth,
a sword in his hand,
hemp fuses smouldering fear
twisted in his beard and hair,
clambering over your gunwale
with those wild eyes
fixed upon your heart, egad;
and they say it took
twenty cutlass slashes,
five pistol shots,
and a slice across the jugular
to slow him down long enough

for Maynard to decapitate 'im,
but that's all right, that's his metier,
he was a *pirate* for chrissake,
                        but that flag —
the poetry of doom ...

W*hat* was he on?

iii.

Accountants, Lawyers, Administrators,
Militarists, Priests, Teachers, Specialists,
Professional Athletes, Talk Show Hosts,
Upper and Lower Management,
Elitists of the World,
Beauty Consultants, Those Who Travel,
Those Who Do Not,
Volunteer Board Presidents,
Phone Solicitors, Politicians omigod,
Incompetents of Every Ilk and Profession,
Publishers, Critics, All the Hierarchies of Hell,
poets ...

This was said to be the meaning of his flag:
"You! All of you! See the hourglass?
Your sand has run out!
Blackbeard's come to pierce your hearts!"
but isn't it far more likely
he knew ... he knew ...

No one is Blackbeard for long, Mr. Teach.

So he hung the image aloft
of what he feared most:
Death looks you in the eye,
the sands of fate in hand,
and when the skeleton rattles your glass
you know you only have
the time left it will take
three drops of your heart's blood
to reach the deck
to take as many as you can
of all the bastards down with you ...
                        Never enough.

Life's Like That

Due to a rare, unfortunate genetic anomaly
brought on by efflorescence
Mr. K's normal personal magnetism
manifested itself in an unseen cloud of electrons
bursting from his body and hovering around his head;
but alas, poor man, instead of having that one vital
extra electron to share
the unfortunate soul
was two electrons beyond a stable octet
(which grouped him with the alkaline earth metals)
and he had to search, to search, to search endlessly
for an impossible match to complete his emotional circuitry,
a woman not one but two electrons short of a charge —

(when all along, unknown to fate
and the hydroelectric board there lived
in the apartment below Mr. K's a ravishing pair
of French positively charged sororal twins,
but their orbits always took them out the front door
while his took him out the back, never in synch)

— the irony of ions.

Points of Viewing

Finally driven screaming from the world
he sought refuge in the only safe haven he knew:
the television: but hugging it was no longer enough.
He kicked out the tube, smashed out the bottom,
and lowered it over his head. Immediately he felt —

Glib. Well-coifed. Less significant than a half-articulated cliché.
He had never been so happy, nor understood less why.
He sang, he danced, he laughed, he —

was a Talent.

"Who da man? I da man!"
She had some trouble adjusting to his new image.
The knobs were in a different place than she was used to.
But eventually she admitted the colour was better,
the relationship far less demanding.
She knew when to leave him alone now,
because she could always wait for a commercial,
and thanks to the laugh track
she always knew when he was trying to be funny.
Then suddenly — harmony!

"Why not?" she thought. She hooked up her VCR,
set him up to tape for later and changed the channel.

Stored in a dark place, with no demands upon him
except to be seen only when she wanted to see him
he had never felt so complete, so appreciated, so ...

Secure.

Indistinctly Extinct

Very subtle, yet the clues are there.

The massive stranger with his back to you,
a field of overcoat, standing halfway
down the crowded bus, so no one can
"move to the back, please ... "

The inconsiderate coworker, unseen,
emptying the coffee pot in a single gulp,
not brewing more, leaving the cream out
to sour, the sugar spilled all over ...

The elusive neighbor, with the perfectly
cropped lawn, who whenever you're away
seems to be leaning over your back fence
and eating the tops off your trees ...

The couple in the ancient evening wear,
too much jewelry, too much perfume,
sitting in the row before you at the opera,
backs like garbage dumpsters
completely blocking the stage,
rattling candy papers in all the quiet spots ...

The dinosaurs have not died out,
they're merely in disguise.

Magic Show

begins with his cape, a strange steely blue
on the outside, red richness beyond belief on the inside,
smooth beyond satin, that when added to the ridiculously thin
stovepipe black top hat and moustaches sticking out
at least six inches on either side of his face,
the logical, irrefutable, scientific fact must be acknowledged,
he looks so good it must be magic.

continues with her assistant's costume,
flaring all over what looked good before,
bottomed by fishnets elevated by nine inch
black stiletto heels, so she towers over him
like an incredibly sensual, black,
sexually predatory beetle, an effect balanced
only by the stupid blue feather she wears in her hair.

There are props, there is music, there is a stageful of shadows,
he yells magical commands with authority, shakes his wand,
she shouts back all the appropriate monosyllables,
and before they know it, they're knee deep in rabbits.

The performance goes on for hours. Exhausted, on the final trick,
his judgement lapses for just one second, the saw slips
and oh, calamity! Off comes her head. He panics.
The saw slips again, and oh, jehosaphat! Off comes his head, too.
Confused, alarmed, good at magic but not at juggling, stovepipe
and feather
shoot up into the air, hang there a moment, staring wildly into
each other's eyes,
then plop down — on the wrong necks.

So he sees him with his eyes but her body
and she sees her with her eyes but his body

so now she knows and she slaps him hard but that means
she hits her own cheek so he hits his cheek to play fair
but he knows now she's really flattered so he tries something improper
and she tries to put him back in his proper place but that means
what should be proper certainly isn't and the panic grows
the saw comes out again and they're hacking off arms, breasts, genitalia,
noses, lips, tongues, mixing and matching until all that's left
are the eyes pleading, put it all right again!
And by magic they do — there's a pause.

They look at each other. Blush.

"Like your cape."

"Like your shoes."

The crowd goes ape.

The higher one climbs on Mount Everest, the more oxygen deprivation affects one's perceptions and capabilities. Nevertheless, climbing Mount Everest has become the "in" thing, especially if you can be the first of your increasingly idiosyncratic set to do so.

Climbing Mount Everest With a Blonde Supermodel Spanish Mathematician

I was only along
for the fluid in the lungs
but she soared
on a psychomountain high.

Discussion began
while we crawled in terror
over three lightly-lashed
aluminum ladders tipped across
a three-mile deep crevasse
in the Kumbu Ice Falls;
a bottomless drop
through 50 below zero
empty space
wonderfully clears the mind.
I never understood her accent
but this is what I think
she said:

      "This equilibrium is inadequate!
One must be true
to a coordinated, pastel,
particular philosophy,
fashionably elegant yet functional
under conditions of reduced oxygen!
Don't find more accurate answers,
pose better problems

to unclutter the complexities
that litter the real world!
Enrich is a good word."

By the time we reached
the Lhotse Face
and the atmosphere thinned
even further I could only reply:

"Logically, one should be
consistently inconsistent
in justifying one's coherence.
To achieve a useful status
be intelligible, plausible,
and most of all fruitful.
Disequilibrium is adequate!"

And then we were
stepping up the Hillary,
oxygen ran out at the pinnacle
of our achievement
and laughing at our success,
we drowned, in unison:

"This is the scaffold
of the prime painter
while he works
to illuminate the ceiling
of the cosmos!
Our sophisticated understanding
of cascading science gives way
to the tinker toys of the infinite!
Over the corpses of frozen heros
we tumble to the top
of transcendence!"

And there we were —
at the summit.
I stop — stunned.
Not from any sense of majesty,
from lack of air.
But my companion
is exultant, having
reached the realization
of a nightmare,
just her and the mountain —
but the mountain doesn't care
so really, just her.
Turning her back to me
and all mankind,
she proclaims:

"Now *I* command God!
Make me one with all!
Make it so!
I am all over
this f-ing continent!"

So I pushed her off.

Tympanic Zen Brain

We found the halcyon bones
of the backstage bandit
filling the cameo ballroom —
then the crowd arrives
whispering of mirrors
of hoodoo cayenne,
emphatic extract
from the midnight feast
halted discretely
by the spectral caress
of spirits walking among us.
We could tell
by the empathic jimjams
reminding us of
unaccountable virtues
we long believed lost
behind smoking mirrors.

Light the rebel beacon,
signal the fustian fandango
and we will two-step
our orbicular nocturne.
Moonbones press tight against me
as you nightbloom
and I taste your lips
and thighs, reminiscent
of hemlock uncertainty.

There is a forgotten entrance.
I find my way again
as you lead me
through private portals.
With a hidden eye

you reveal a ruby sanctum,
the door an iron shriek
opening to reveal our
suddenly tragic hour.
The whimsical zombie
revels over our
hesitant zeitgeist.

Once more
we
          sink back
     into the
     gaudy silhouette
     of the
          every day
               tableau ...

There Must Be A Punchline

What do I take
from the deeds of Mankind,
supreme monster of grace?
A year-long rhapsody
never to be defeated,
to be crowned in a ring
of paralyzing, surprising joy
over the moment
he threw fire in the eyes
of the large and momentous;
the fire of grace and conflict
bursting from the earth
a tattooed dream of astonishment,
with a superhuman, monumental effort —
but more than that.
What watcher may judge
the beauty of impossible odds?

Lost after all these years
of treachery, deception,
the bell tolls for thee, Mankind —
not good versus evil.
I often cheered for evil.
In the beautiful, mystic rhythm,
a perfect sense of balance.
Now so rarely do I leap from my chair
threatened by the monster, Mankind.
There are no rude monsters
so beautiful as he,
or the rhapsody that soothed him.

All the tattered warriors streaming,
Leave them now.
There must be a punchline.

Anubis on the Prairies

a vast expanse, green, yellow, and blue ...
then the lonely buildings merge,
and He is there, black,
crouching in the distance

Traveling far across the flat, flat land,
I could not ignore the obvious —
nothing can really be that empty.
I fill the sky with visions,
and a great voice rings out:

"There are too many bloody annoying people
needing a swift guiding kick to the afterlife!"

Rising out of the prairie tall grass
He strides gigantic, spanning the countryside —
the ancient Black Death Dog of Egypt.
Surely his words do not pertain to me.
Surely he is not cursing my soul
when the numbers are so enormous to choose from.
Can He not see I am too small
beneath this yellow sun?

I awake,
return to futile conversation,
and desperately try to enable meaning.

deus ex vampira

When I was young and hairier,
and I caught that first hint
that all of life would not remain
so sweet and rosy as I naively dreamed,
the shadows grew thick,
I despaired and cried aloud in anguish,
and in overwhelming response to my pain,
no one answered.

How was an untrodden lad of tender sensibility
to cope? My vision of a life so kind, so fair in every way
shattered by the hard grind of reality; compassion and caring
exposed as the pale, marshmallow fantasies they were,
I dreamed of only one recourse:
Become a vampire, and suck the bastards dry!

But, such a step smacked of implausibility —
too convenient, too just to be a true aesthetic fit —
and alas, was abandoned,
with the other innocent effects of childhood.
Engulfed by the petty parasites
that do comprise this world.

And I grew older, wiser, balder ...

But an undead dream does not die.
The inner me will yet arise, tall, gaunt,
nobly arrayed in opera cloak and tails,
hissing heavily accented clichés of power,
staring down critics with meaningful,
compelling, bat-winged eyes, damming forever
the slow, mundane drain of the everyday leech,
and miraculously, not a hair out of place.

Not a joke. Not a hoax. Not a toupee. Truly,
fangs with panache.

Hot Fish Music

Down at the Whalebone Inn the hot cats of the ocean play
a tune I've not heard the rhythms like beat
from any sane dude's drum the Scrimshaw Quartet
with their calcium reeds and knucklebone tympani
slide it in sideways sharp as a fishgutter's knife
filleting you in five/four time sending your innards
slipping across the floor and oh the dance you do
to keep up with the evil wicked wicked teasing your ear
the hottest cat wails and all the whales are hot cats too
until the full weight of their downbeat tides you,
sinks you to the bottom and once you forget how to breathe
           oh, then you're in trouble,
           then you're in tune
           then
           you're in love.

Standing Mast-Head

Too much! The sharks are snapping more than circling
the only way out is to climb high enough to see my life
barreling in on every side and barreling away on every other;
in deep concentration then I find the rigging and hoist myself aloft!
Despite winds that blow and a mast-head too high to see
I climb, hand over hand, foot above foot, onwards to upwards,
all thought of the fray below lost in the struggle to remain above
— focus is all. I climb beyond madness, beyond weariness, beyond
strength.
At just the moment I forget entirely what I am climbing for
the mast-head comes in view. I cannot resist a pause,
a surprised smile of triumph, a moment of distraction
— I am lost. A fatal mistake — to look down from such a height,
to see there is more to the sea than just my own ship,
to be hypnotized by the ocean. The dark, blue, heaving,
rolling, eternal ... motion. I see the vast gulfs
between my ship and every other, the endless horizons
on every side; I hear ... The motion has sound.
I close my eyes and listen to the rhythm as alive
as the movement —

                             and never see the whale

ramming my ship

                             sending me flying into infinity.

The Cinnamon Whale

I pick my crew carefully,
no strong backs, but enough imagination between 'em
to spear the moon and sink it in a teacup,
Vida at the helm, Strong Ron in the stern,
Peter Paul, P.B., and Friesen picking up the slack,
every pen a massive oar but my own,
the deadly, barbed harpoon.
We lower, and away! After the red whale.
The breeze is fresh, the water energetic
in wave and flow seeking to rock us over one moment,
to propel us spear forward the next.
The whale runs hot before us —
its tail blocks out the sun,
one enormous fan of lead-weight bamboo
ready to sink us as soon as cool us.
But there's none so cool as us today —
I shift to the bow, set my stance,
harpoon at the ready — what is the whale?
Certainly not a fish, not a mammal,
not on the edge of extinction as Melville denied,
this is the whale of strong appeal,
of heavily-scented adventure, a whale
of a different flavour that we pursue
without blood, without slaughter,
without frightening imposition of sanity
upon a natural world deserving so much better,
this is the whale that can only be speared,
only be shaped, by the imagination,
and we are the only crew alive today
who even try to catch it —
I toss the steel! A hit! We ride the wild ride!
The white water rages as we cut through the waves
in the wake of the whale!

We try to control it, we try to drag it down,
but its power runs away with us; with mad laughter now
we'll happily drown, suddenly aware
as sharp as our irons are, as clearly they cut
our every word, the whale will never be slowed,
will never be caught, will never be tied down
even by the likes of us — we can only live to hunt,
never to slaughter —

the whale rears and turns,
crashes down upon our all too fragile craft
and our all too groping souls —
with loud and happy cheers, knowing all delight,
we explode in a cloud of fragrant spice
and throw all our pens at once,
arcing against the sun in the bright blue sky ...

The Ancient Sands of Egypt

Beneath this sun, I cannot be —
begin to fall, to crumble, to drift ...

fine, infinitely grained,
wind-tossed,
almost liquid, living ...

beyond thought,
slow as the desert
moving towards the tomb.

Ages pass. Another joins me.

In the shadow of the grave,
regaining form
we are lovers until the sunrise.

Then, the 5000 gods of Egypt
render us sand once more
but mixed ...

each infinite grain
loving just as profoundly
each other infinite grain

as did the whole

as all the ages of man
pass by with a last, gentle

sigh ...

teaching her how to fly

on the grassy cliff, above the deep, deep sea
I adjust her harness, show her where the release is,
give her a quick kiss and a laugh, and then back up,
to get a good running start ...
                    Both of us naked,
she climbs upon my shoulders and I lurch forward,
leaning, using her weight to overcome inertia, building
momentum,
feet moving faster, feeling the first puff of lift, lessening weight,
I tear for the edge and we are away!

Dropping like a stone, but she calms, lets me go,
                    the upgust catches her canvas,
and she soars! Flying upwards towards the sun.
I dagger into the sea, piercing deep into the murk,
regain balance, stroke to the surface, my head emerges
gasping, in time to watch her go ...
                    sailing, receding, against but with the sky.
Ever more distant, yet singing to me with a joy
more intense by the moment.

My heart lifts with hers to know now she knows
she had it, she could do it, she not only deserved to
she did it, she can fly.

With easy, happy strokes, I set out across the sea
to our rendezvous.

Dr. Hoffman's Happy Gene Machine

Inert with fatigue and pain,
I lie immobile casting my mind outward;
nothing — then inward. Abruptly, all hinges
on one dimly remembered melody ...

I follow the memory until I stand alone
in the dark, on one side of calm waters.
On the other, the ineluctable siren calls.
I cast a coin upon the water.

The grinning ferryman materializes,
awkwardly poking forward a craft
he has no skill for — he's drunk.
A lanky imp, balding in furs and pince nez,
butting his boat against my bank.
Teetering on the edge, I clamber into his arms;
we tumble, shipping water, tippling onwards
to Dr. Hoffman's Palace of Delight ...

Somewhere in our hazy sense of movement,
we lose the siren
but the Doctor himself greets us at the door.
In moments, we dwell in light and colour,
our glasses never empty. Shouting their delight,
mechanical women drop from the air,
a line of spring-loaded dancing girls
in frolicking ruffles kicking high enough
for both they and we three leering fools

to defy gravity. The music, now a physical force,
propels us across the floor, we join the dance!
Arm in arm and drunk enough at last
we sing and kick blind to all consequences
right out the door, past the point marked "No Return",
and laugh, falling headlong into the abyss ...

But as we go, from high above,
once more we hear the siren sing,
darkly reassuring, compelling our utter faith
in love.
                And then we fly.

Compulsion

Knowing that, for whatever reason,
I must, I simply must haul this block of marble
to the top of that cliff
and hurl with it nude to my death
on whatever irregular surface lies below,
I resolve the process must be rendered
worthy of both my effort and attention.
Having learnt from bitter experience
that squared meters of hard stone
are neither simple nor fun
to lug about on my naked back,
but that a naked woman
with outstretched arms
is another matter entirely,
I begin to carve.
I use only the warmth of my hands,
the fever of my compulsion,
and the stone melts like butter.
I mold and shape my unfathomable burden.
When complete, I gain an easy grip,
and we climb, arriving all too soon
at the point of earthly departure.
I get ready to shove her over the edge —
but — alas, I have built too well.
My fever runs too high,
there must be a proper farewell
or at least a simple introduction,
before we leave this veil forever.
I drape myself upon her and kiss,
kiss her silent, cold, stone lips

as I have never kissed
any set of lips before —
animal, vegetable, or mineral.
The heat begins to pass from my body
into hers, she quickens, she lives,
She Lives! We will escape our inexorable doom —
Nope. Her newly vibrant arms
clutch me to her ample bosom,
I lose my balance, and oh hell
over we go. But, oh look!

The afternoon is just full of surprises,
because after we resolve
while unconnected to all and sundry
to enjoy the utter abandonment
of ardour in free flight
before the pull of gravity
so rudely reasserts itself,
and we are just about to consummate
our now completely mutual fever —
SPLASH! There's a freaking freezing lake
at the bottom of the cliff,
quenching ardour, abandon, fever,
and a huge percentage
of our common cosmic consciousness ...

Gasping, we haul ourselves to shore
and collapse on the sand,
half in, half out of the water.
Exhausted, we drowse,
face to face, our bodies, our lips,
our souls, ever so close to each other
but not quite touching ...
But I can't sleep.
There is a calm, flowing ripple
ebbing and surging directly between

our naked bodies, closer each moment
to where our hearts almost meet,
our hands almost touch.
The surge heaves entirely within our shadow
except for one spark of sunshine,
an uneasy window of crystal light.
I stare at the rippling gleam,
and again, my fever builds, a wild compulsion —
then I'm gone.
No more body, only me transformed
into the sparkle on the water
at the exact moment she opens her eyes
and sees the gleam
for the first and only time —
She captures me.
Now and forevermore
just a happy memory,
the sparkle in her eye,
urging her on to ever more
and madder desire.

Destination Mutable

Facing a black and silent canyon
I know there is a place for me beyond.
I must span the void with a golden bridge
but the only stones I have to work with
are words — and words are oh so heavy.
Each block must be chosen to perfectly fit the last.
I must carve each step forward precisely
from a mass that does not care for precision.
Still, I move onward. I progress one step, then another.
And each step forward leads to another
until slowly the gap is closed. Each new word falls faster,
clearer in meaning, more certain into place.
I stride the bridge, proud and confident
— abruptly the end is in sight. I pause —
for a moment, to appreciate, not just to abandon, the silent void.
But I am startled from my contemplation,
as the woman I thought waited before me,
compelling my building onward, approaches from behind.
She binds my eyes with sparkling laughter,
takes my hand, and leads me off — not forward.
Not backwards. To one side, where I have placed no words.
I expect to plummet, but instead journey on,
supported by I will never know what ...

When the blindfold is removed, I am lying naked on a bed
on a high plateau of light, somewhere in the void,
the sheets so cool and perfect white beneath me.
My lover caresses me with the soft torrent tangles of her hair ...

Afterwards, she sleeps, face down, but I lie alert,
growing more certain of my destination.
Out of the void I levitate one perfect fresh rose,
dark green stem dripping three moist light-filled drops
cool along my lover's back, beginning just below the waist ...
I bring the rose before me, and stare into its deep,
deep crimson ... and do not think or trust to words.

She awakes, to find only the rose beside her.
She leans softly back, smiles,
and lays the flower
between her breasts.

Waking Up Gautama

Enlightened by a dream,
I could not help
but be happy

one day.

Other Green Frigate Books

In Print:

Healing Natures, Repairing Relationships: New Perspectives on Restoring Ecological Spaces and Consciousness
Robert L. France

A Wanderer All My Days: John Muir in New England
J. Parker Huber

Ultreia! Onward! Progress of the Pilgrim
Robert Lawrence France

Wetlands of Mass Destruction:
Ancient Presage for Contemporary Ecocide in Southern Iraq
Robert Lawrence France

Liquid Gold: The Lore and Logic of Using Urine to Grow Plants (First Edition)
Carol Steinfeld

Profitably Soaked: Thoreau's Experience of Water
Robert Lawrence France

Deep Immersion: The Experience of Water
Robert Lawrence France

Uncommon Cents: Thoreau and the Nature of Business
Robert M. Abbott

Forthcoming:

Conscious Endeavors: Business, Society and the Journey to Sustainability
Robert M. Abbott

Zombie Factory: A Cross-Cultural and Interdisciplinary Perspective on the Communication of Stress
Michael A. Korovkin and Peter H. Stephenson

The Eight Pillars of a Sustainable Community
Mark Holland

Weather Patterns: Climate, Culture, and Place Making
Allan W. Shearer

GREEN FRIGATE BOOKS

"THERE IS NO FRIGATE LIKE A BOOK"

Words on the page have the power to transport us, and in the process, transform us. Such journeys can be far reaching, traversing the land- scapes of the external world and that within, as well as the timescapes of the past, present and future.

Green Frigate Books is a small publishing house offering a vehicle—a ship—for those seeking to conceptually sail and explore the horizons of the natural and built environments, and the relations of humans within them. Our goal is to reach an educated lay readership by producing works that fall in the cracks between those offered by traditional academic and popular presses.